Success
A 12 Step
Program

Jody N Holland

ISBN: 0-9839835-8-5
ISBN-13: 978-0-989835-8-3

DEDICATION

This book is dedicated to the people who helped me get back up each time that I got knocked down in life. It is dedicated to the people who believed in me and stood by me as I kept attempting to accomplish something great. I am thankful to have friends and family that knew that there was always a next step for me.

CONTENTS

ACKNOWLEDGMENTS

I would like to acknowledge anyone who told me that I couldn't succeed in life. To my second grade teacher, I say thank you for making me, and a host of other 7-year olds, angry. You told us we were stupid and worthless. Even though no teacher who is worth the air they breathe would ever do what you did, it motivated me to prove you to be an idiot. It has been my struggles and my nay-sayers that have incited my intense drive for success.

I would also like to acknowledge all the people who supported and encouraged me. You helped me to remember that the negative people in the world could not bring me down unless I allowed them to do so. It was all of the experiences that I interpreted, yes interpreted, in my life that have lead to my overcoming the challenges of life and moving through the 12-Steps of Success.

Introduction

In life, we have choices. We have the choice to push ourselves to our limits. We have the choice to be lazy. We have the choice to be balanced. We have the choice to define our success or to allow others to twist their definition into our psyche. The tough part is not what to choose. That seems easy to define what people think they want. The tough part is to accept the fact that it is a choice. In a course through my Buddy-2-Boss Series, titled Corrective Counseling, you learn that one of our human needs is to explain the reasoning behind why things happen in our lives. When something happens... we ask why. There are only two explanations that are relevant. We either explain what happened as something that was inside of our control, or something that was outside of our control. That's it! If it is internally attributed, then we made a choice. We had a say in the outcome and could have made it different than it was if we had chosen to do so. If it is externally attributed, then it was outside of our control and we were without a say or a choice in the matter.

I have found that there really is very little that is outside of our control completely. There are things that other people do that we did not have a choice in. However, once they make a choice, we are not without a choice ourselves. We can still determine what our next move will be. We get to choose our attitudes at work, in relationships, in life. The attitude that we choose will determine the way that we process events and ultimately the way that we make our next choices in any given situation. The "Attribution Theory" is pretty clear. We explain everything in our life either internally or externally. My observation is that most people attribute the good stuff internally and the bad stuff externally.

By doing so, we assume that when good things happen, we had a lot to do with it and when bad things happen, there must have been some unseen force that was hijacking our dream. This is a defeatist's mentality. This is putting you in a position of weakness and helplessness. It is not a good place to be. Feeling defeated and feeling that you have no control can lead to sadness, anger, and ultimately depression.

I once heard depression defined as anger without the enthusiasm. I don't honestly want to be angry, or unenthusiastic. I want to be in a position of success. I want to be in a position where I take control of my present and therefore create my future. I don't want to simply throw my hands up and let life happen to me. I want to make life happen.

Don't get me wrong. I do believe that there are things that can be outside of our control. I don't believe that if I simply think the right way that my life will be perfect. I do, however, believe that if I think the right way, I will be much better prepared to handle the bumps in the road that come with living life. I want to be the success that I dream of. That means, that I have to be willing to be in the fight. I have to step into the arena and be willing to get my butt kicked in order to have the chance to also be on top of the world.

I remember learning that lesson as a 9-year old in martial arts. I would step quickly out of the ring when someone would attack in a sparring match because I was afraid of getting hit. I didn't want to get hurt. After doing this for a couple of weeks, my instructor made me fight without using my hands or scooting back at all until I was willing to take a hit. I got progressively better until I was 13 years old and started working out with a kick-boxer. I learned to really take a punch or a kick at that point. It was really amazing that getting hit was a little invigorating at times. It was amazing that once I was really willing to take a punch, people became scared of me. They would back away from anyone that was willing to lose.

That lesson has served me well in business. There are very few people in this world that are actually willing to lose. There are few that are willing to risk it all and see what happens. **My belief is that success, money, and victory are formed in the mind and then they materialize in our world through the conduit of action.** Action is the bridge that makes the unseen become real. Don't ever miss that piece of the success puzzle. Without action, you have nothing but empty dreams and hope. That, my friend, is not a strategy.

This book is a series of steps that I have found to be necessary to take in order to achieve success in life. If you are unwilling to take the correct steps, then you are not willing to do what is necessary to achieve success. I fashioned the title after AA's programs. The 12 Step Program in Alcoholics Anonymous is one of the most successful behavior change and results change systems ever written. These are obviously not the same steps, but I wanted to make the connection to the symbolism. These steps are about creating the right pattern of behaviors to succeed.

As you read the book, I strongly encourage you to do the exercises that are associated with each chapter. By doing so, you will create the strongest likelihood of success for yourself. Ultimately, being successful, or winning in life is about knowing what to do and then doing it. It is not about knowing what to do and hoping something happens. It is not about waiting until the right people know you. It is about taking action and introducing yourself into the right circles. It is about being the right person that others can't help but know.

I wish you all the best on your journey to success!

Jody N Holland - Fellow Journeyer

1 DEFINE YOUR CURRENT REALITY AND COME TO GRIPS WITH IT

The first step is always the hardest. The truth is that we often want to think of ourselves as the person who is doing everything that we can do in order to be successful. If the economy was better, if we had a different leader, if our company would do better marketing, if, if, if, then we would be in that place of success. It is not our fault that we are who we are and where we are. All those statements do is ensure that you will stay in the place that you're in now. I would imagine you picked up this book in order to make sure that you got to the place you wanted to be, not to stay in the place that you already are.

So, here I go... My name is Jody and I am a fofnoficator.

Definition

Fofnoficator - a person who has a fear of failure and therefore has a tendency to put off showing his work to the rest of the world out of fear of what they might think of it.

I said it. I said what has held me back. Just like making any other change in our lives, we have to first define who and where we actually are.

If you are unwilling to be honest with yourself right here, right now, then you will stay in this version of your life. Keep in mind, you can be anybody that you want to be, but you have to know where you are starting.

When I was 15 years old, my father took a job in Abilene, TX, moving our family about 5 hours from where I had lived since the summer before 2nd grade. This was a big move, but an exciting one. I was excited because I realized at the moment that my father told us about it that I would have a chance to redefine myself. I had come to terms with the image I had of myself and the image I had allowed others to have of me, but I didn't like it. I knew what image I wanted for myself. So, I intentionally created the new me when I moved during my Sophomore year in high school. I did that because I did not like what I had created and wanted to create something new.

As I write this, I am thinking about who the current "me" really is.

I am an entrepreneur that has spent an inordinate amount of time feeling like I need someone to help me be successful.

I am a writer who loves to get my thoughts on paper, but is afraid of putting them out to the masses for fear of their negative reviews.

I am a sales person who worries about the rejection that can happen in the sales process and often takes the easy road and just has a conversation instead.

I am a person who knows exactly what to do in order to be successful, but chooses not to do what is required. Instead, I often do menial tasks to fill my time, knowing that they will not help.

Wow! That felt a little like getting my butt kicked...by me! I, just like you, have to come to grips with what I am doing that is holding me back from the level of success that I know I can attain. I want you to take a minute and write out 3 to 5 realities of who you are and how it is keeping you from attaining the success you have espoused that you want.

_____

_____

_____

_____

_____

_____

_____

_____

My belief, and the belief of a number of self-help gurus out there is that success begins in your mind, specifically in what I would call your residual self-definition.

You have a subconscious blue-print for success, failure, or mediocrity. It is based on the programming that you have enabled and even endorsed in your mind. You have allowed stimuli into your subconscious via your conscious mind that has shaped you into the person that you are right now. It is the programming that has to change. My very first computer programming class in college talked about this very thing. My professor said, garbage in, garbage out. It is not the code. It is the coder. Code only does what you tell it to do. It has no emotion or feeling tied up in behaving in a certain manner. It only carries out what it was instructed to do. Your subconscious is that software code for your life. What is it that you have told it to do?

_____

_____

_____

_____

_____

_____

_____

_____

2 SURROUND YOURSELF WITH RIGHT-MINDED PEOPLE

Step 2 is to surround yourself with the right minded people. It is absolutely amazing how long people will stay in toxic relationships. Whether it be a business relationship or a personal one, staying with someone who simply drags you down makes no sense. I don't want to come across as callous or uncaring, because I am not. I do want to be clear, though, that the people who are around you will have a tremendous influence on your psychological state.

If you are working with someone whom you don't or simply can't trust, then that person has to go from your life. Don't spend your time worrying about what you are losing. Instead, spend your time focusing on who you should be and who you can be. Think back to what your mother, or father, used to say to you when you were young. "Be careful who you hang out with! You will become like them." If you hang out with unethical people, you will eventually do things that you know are unethical. Rationalization becomes the easy way out. If you hang out with people who are unsuccessful, you will eventually become unsuccessful.

When I think about the person I want to be, I begin looking for people who exhibit those characteristics. I begin looking for people who have a high moral standard, who operate with clear ethical guidelines. I look for people who have achieved the level of success that I want to achieve, or greater. I look for people that embody the place that I want to be.

I remember thinking at one point, as I was struggling to find success, that I wanted to read a story about someone who was like I was at one time, unsuccessful. I wanted to know that I was not alone. The realization hit me very quickly that they don't write stories about people who fail, people who quit, or people who don't apply the readily available success principles. They write stories about people who push the limits and define their own brand of success.

The first thing that you have to do in order to accomplish step 2 is to define the attributes that you want to mirror. So, let's take a moment and write out what those characteristics are. Fill in the blanks below with the attributes and why each attribute is important to you. I have provided an example on the top line.

Attribute   Why This Is A Must For Me

Example: Balance
Balance is a must for me because to have true success, it must be in all domains of life, not just money, or not just physical health.

_____

_____

_____

_____

_____

_____

_____

_____

_____

The next phase is to identify people who have each of the attributes that you wish to emulate / model. Take a few minutes and write down the names of people that you think possess the qualities you want to demonstrate. It does not matter if they are alive or dead. It can be famous people, a relative, or simply someone you know or have known. Re-write the attribute and then put the person's name and short description of how they demonstrate the attribute.

Attribute: Person And How They Demonstrate The Attribute

_____

_____

_____

_____

_____

_____

_____

_____

_____

_____

The next step is to find out ways to learn more about those people, their choices, their behaviors, and their belief systems. You see, our underlying beliefs lead to our thoughts. Our thoughts lead to our feelings. Our feelings lead to our actions. And, our actions lead to our results. If you want to change your results, you need to go all the way back to what you believe. It is very possible that if you want to be rich, yet you think that rich people are stuck up snobs and you don't like stuck up snobs, that you are the root cause of not being rich. If you think back to your childhood, you will see that you were "programmed" to think in a certain way. This happens by spending time with a certain person or group of people.

If you want to change that underlying programming, which is the only way to change your results, then you need to modify your inputs. By learning about people who are successful, related to your definition of success, then you will learn what and how they believe so that you can begin adopting the same belief patterns. Pay close attention. You will become what you think about continuously... good or bad. If you are surrounded by negative people, you will become negative and you will get negative results. If you surround yourself with successful people, you will become successful and you will get positive results.

Seek out biographies, networking groups, training videos, seminars, dvd's and whatever else you can get your hands on. If you do this, you will find that you become like minded and ultimately right minded.

The final exercise I have for you in this chapter is this. Pick the one person from your above list that most resembles who and what you want to be. Then, write out why you absolutely MUST become like them. What are the benefits of becoming like them? And then, what are the consequences of not becoming like them. After you write this out, I want you to call someone you trust and tell them about this person, why you want to be like them and what it will cost you to not become like them.

The person that most resembles who I want to be in life is _____. The benefits of me becoming like this person are...

_____

_____

_____

_____

_____

_____

_____

_____

_____

_____

The consequences for not taking action, learning about this person, and becoming like them are...

_____

_____

_____

_____

_____

_____

_____

_____

_____

The goal you should have is to continuously learn from people who have made it to where you want to be. Never surround yourself with people that are at your level or below. Seek to surround yourself with people that are significantly beyond where you are at this moment. Then, strive to be at or above their level. When I was lifting weights in high school, I used to love working out with people that could bench press more than I could. I found that when I worked out with them, I would give significantly more effort. When I worked out with people that I was already stronger than, I would give only the amount of effort that was required. I don't want to be the person who only does what is necessary to get by. I want to be the person that changes the world because I gave all that I had to offer and lived as if I was moving up. I learned from the best, and surrounded myself with people that could and would push me. If you want to be a millionaire, you need to hang out with millionaires. If you want to be track star, you need to hang out with track stars. You become what you think about continuously! You become who you hang around continuously because those are the people who influence your thought. Choose your inputs wisely! You may even need to choose to hang around people that are beyond your level of achievement.

So the question would be... What are those characteristics that you need in people around you in order to be successful? I heard it said once that if you want to be a millionaire, then you need to find some deca-millionaires to hang out with. Wherever you would like to be, find people that are already beyond that and find ways to be around them. The simple process of engaging with those successful people will stimulate something in your mind that will help you see the path to success. Some of the characteristics of successful people that seem to be very common are as follows.

1. Successful people look for ways to maximize their return on investment with anything that they do. Unsuccessful people focus on not wanting to work too hard, or ensuring that they just stay secure. Maximizing your return on investment often involves learning to leverage the talent of others who are not willing to take risks the way you are. You don't go into business for yourself or push for that next level up with the hopes of getting out of the venture just what you put into it. You should have the objective of at least tripling your return. Look for ways that you can continuously make more money with less of your time required. That is maximizing your return on investment.

2. Successful people go to market. Unsuccessful people will always find a couple of more things that need to be done before they put themselves out there. Never be afraid to put your work out there for others to see. The reality is that it may be amazing work in the mind of others when it is only good in your mind. There is a tremendous respect for people who are willing to go to market. It is always better to take imperfect action than it is to take no action. You have zero chance of success if

you never go to market. You have a decent chance
of success if it is at least out there. So, in the words
of a friend of mine... "Quit your danged infernal
tinkering and do something!"

3. Successful people get rid of those things and
people who drag them down. Unsuccessful people
hold on to the toxic relationships. Unsuccessful
people do this in order to make themselves feel
better. When they are around people whose lives
are worse than theirs, they feel better. They are able
to say, "Look at them. At least I am not that bad."
Successful people identify those relationships
quickly and eliminate them. It does not matter if it
is an employee or a personal relationship, they get
rid of the folks in their lives that are toxic, the ones
that drag them down. Go out of your way to stay
away from negative people.

4. Successful people are not intimidated by
successful or rich or happy or fully engaged people.
Unsuccessful people resent those who are doing
better than they are. I believe that at a base level of
thought, we resent what intimidates us. I believe
that is why unsuccessful people think so poorly of
the people who are doing great in life. Successful
people look at those who are doing better than they
are and say, "Wow, look at how great they are
doing. I wonder what I can learn from them?"
Successful people look up to those who are doing
better than they are and find ways to emulate what
they are doing that is working.

5. Successful people never stop learning and never feel that they know it all. Unsuccessful people believe that they know all they need to know and refuse to be open minded to learning new things. You know the type that I am talking about. They are the ones that use phrases like "that'll never work" and "we tried that before and it didn't work" as their answer to virtually every idea. Successful people look at challenges and ask themselves what they would have to learn in order to be successful at overcoming the challenge. Successful people make learning a part of their every day requirement. The top 1% intellectually in the U.S. will read one new book a month for personal development. I don't know about you, but I like putting myself in that category. Education, growth, and learning are major priorities for successful people. I was told in college, as an English Minor, that I was not well read on a subject until I had read at least 100 books on the topic. Having read more than 100 books on leadership and success, I would say that there are at least 100 more that I need to read now.

6. Successful people are willing to grind away the hours because they know that hard work is a part of their success. Mark Twain once said, "The harder I work, the luckier I get." I truly believe that anyone who says that you will not have to put in hours to be successful will lie about other stuff too. The difference is that when you are doing what you love, it really doesn't feel like work at all. Work becomes play. It is enjoyable and engaging. You often have trouble with NOT working because you

enjoy what you are doing so much. Unsuccessful people watch the clock. They are there to trade time for money, not results for money. They focus on when they get to leave. Successful people focus on when they get to arrive again.

7. Successful people compete. Unsuccessful people are afraid of competition. Competition is the cornerstone of capitalism. Most entrepreneurs thrive on this competition. They get excited about the idea of trying to crush a competitor. They get chills running down their spine when it is time to enter the battlefield of business on a Monday morning and see if they can walk out as the victor. They are not afraid of a fight. They are not afraid of competition. In fact, the competition brings out the best in them. It pushes them to perform at their highest level. Unsuccessful people will simply cower at the thought of having to compete against someone who is bigger, better funded, or more seasoned than they are. Successful people stand tall, get their footing, and go headfirst into the battle.

When you begin to look at what you consider to be successful, what are the characteristics or behaviors that you can observe? Are the people you look up to hard workers? Are they dedicated? Are they creative? What are the things that you define as success in others? You need to be clear on these things in order to see the world clearly. If you don't define what you want, you will find yourself surrounded with very vague people. Those are the people who will not push you forward, who will not lead you, and who will not help you. Define what the best looks like.

The reason that country clubs are popular for up and coming executives is that successful people are already there. You have to go where the best are. Whether or not you join a country club is up to you. The best are at coffee shops, at church, at Chamber of Commerce events, on the golf course, at the bank, and at a host of other places. The key is that you have to go where they are in order to engage with them. You cannot wait for someone to discover you. Instead, discover them and be willing to prove that you will work to succeed like they have. Successful people go out of their way to help others who also wish to be successful. They are there to help you as long as you are not arrogant or resentful.

If you are unwilling to surround yourself with success, then success will be unwilling to attach itself to you.

3 DEFINE YOUR FUTURE

People continuously indicate that they want a better future than the present one they are experiencing. We want more time with our families. We want more money. We want more freedom. We want a better living condition. The list could go on and on. The reality is that we often don't get what we want because we only know what we don't want, and not what we do want. If you were setting goals within your company and said that you wanted to do better next year than you did this year, that would not mean anything. It doesn't mean anything when you say you want a better living condition either. You have to really take a look at the specifics of what you want, when you want them, and what you are going to give up to get them.

There are five domains of life that you must address. You must define your personal relationships, your financial life, your spiritual life, your physical life, and your psycho-emotional (mental and emotional) life. Your brain has to be able to see and accept the future that you lay out. If you say that you will do 50 million dollars in business and you have never done business before, it is highly unlikely that your subconscious and conscious minds will sync up. Just because you say it out loud does not mean that you will actually accept it. Fake it till you make it only works for getting a date, not for changing your world.

So let's explore a little bit of how the subconscious receives suggestions. Your mind works with images, not words. For this reason, it is critical that you develop the ability to visualize. When you picture your future, you need to be able to see the mental imagery of what the right future looks like. The second factor that must be considered is that your mind thinks in the present, not in the future tense. The third aspect of planning your future is to recognize that you must be willing to give something up in order to get something. Your subconscious has accepted the fact that you must do something in order to get a result. When you put these three factors together, it shapes the way that you would affirm the right future for you. First, you need to get a dream board put together with what you will achieve. A dream board is simply a poster board, or digital collage of pictures that represent your right future. So many people live into the wrong future because they have no vision of what the right future would be. The mistake that many people make on their dream board is to put only the financial goals that they have, or their toy goals.

They want an awesome car, a great house, dream vacations, etc. The challenge is to represent each of the domains equally. Let's look at how you would do that.

Step 1: Write down how you want to feel as a success in each of the domains of life. For example, with your personal relationships in life, how would you define success?

"It is November 14, 2016 and my wife and I are taking a short vacation together. We go out of our way every month to take a night together, just the two of us. This connection is so great for us. We spend hours talking, laughing, dreaming, planning, and enjoying our time together. By taking this time, we have ensured that we are each other's best friend. I trust her completely. I love her deeply. I can't wait to see her at the end of each day. I can't imagine not taking this night every month to simply get away. Two to three times per year, we will take a long weekend together. The mountains are our favorite place to go and simply connect. Every year, my family takes a vacation together. Even though the girls are older now, they still love the time we get to spend together. We talk daily, but still have plenty to discuss when we get to our two weeks away per year. It took a strong commitment to get here, but the sacrifice of time has been absolutely worth it. I can remember the first overnight together. My wife and I were so worried about whether someone was going to call and say that the kids needed something. They didn't. The first long weekend was the same way. The family

vacation had some whining from the kids before we left because they had wanted to be with their friends. However, once we made it to our destination, everything was great! The whining stopped, the smiles appeared, and we all connected. We also gave up eating out as much as we used to. We limited ourselves to one night per week, instead of the three that we used to have. We took the money that we were spending from those other two times out and we put it into the "relationship account" at the bank. We opened this account for this specific reason. Man, has it paid off."

That would be an example of how you would define your relationships. You may want to discuss how you are with your friends, family, coworkers, church family, or other connections. The three keys are to speak in the present tense, paint a mental picture, and define what you are willing to give up in order to achieve these outcomes. As you write it, put down what you gave up. By defining things clearly, your subconscious is simply remembering what it did to create success in that area. What I would like for you to do right now, is practice writing some of this out. For each of the domains listed below, write out what your life "IS" like five years from today. Include how you feel about it because the emotion makes it stick. Paint a picture... in the present tense... with an explanation of what you did to get there.

Personal Relationships: These are your connections with family, friends, and significant individuals in your life.

Financial Life: This portion of your life has to do with your earnings, savings, and monetary success.

Spiritual Life: This portion of your life has to do with your balance in life and your connection to a higher power.

Physical Life: This portion of your life has to do with your physical body, exercise, energy, and how you feel about how you look.

Psycho-Emotional Life: This portion of your life has to do with your mental development and emotional health. You should take into account learning, personal growth, and your emotional well-being.

Remember to look five years down the road from today when you write out how you did over the previous five years. Once you do that, you simply have to remember how you got to where you wanted to be and act on it.

Personal Relationships: _____

_____

_____

_____

_____

_____

_____

_____

_____

_____

Financial Life: _____

_____

_____

_____

_____

_____

_____

_____

_____

_____

Spiritual Life: _____

_____

_____

_____

_____

_____

_____

_____

_____

_____

Physical Life: _____

_____

_____

Psychological-Emotional Life: _____

Now that you have taken the time to write out how you did over a five year period of increased success, let's put some pictures to it. I want you to think about what it looks like to have achieved each of the previous descriptions. Thanks to the internet, you can easily find pictures that match up to what we are seeing in our mind. Use some of the key words from your descriptions to search for the right images of your success. I have found that a physical picture that you see multiple times per day of what your success looks like is the best plan for reinforcing what you are seeking. My suggestion would be to go to your local office store and buy a poster-board that you can mark off into five areas. Each area will represent one of the domains of life that you are defining. I would put the poster-board sideways and have five equal sections with a label at the top of each section. Then, cut out four or five pictures for each area and paste them into the appropriate section. My recommendation is to put the poster-board up where you will see it at least three times per day. This could be in front of your desk, in front of your toilet (you do go there regularly), or beside the door before you walk out of the office or the house. By keeping it in a prominent place, you quickly and easily reinforce the images of your success. Writing out a long affirmation that you read five times a day does not usually happen. If you are given even three minutes of information to read, it becomes easy for people to skip over it in a hurry. The images sink in instantly to your mind without any tedious reading or perceived "work" to do.

Once you have finished the project, write out what it was like for you to do this. Specifically, what benefit do you intend to gain by putting together a collage of your success?

_____

_____

_____

_____

_____

_____

_____

_____

_____

Take the time to do the things that make you successful. I know that some people will look at these things and shrug them off. I also know that some people will do each of the steps correctly. If you are willing to do what it takes, heaven and earth will move to accommodate your vision of where you want to be in life. People will come into your life and work for you without you even asking.

You simply have to have a strong vision in your mind and the willingness to take action. Nothing happens for the person who is unwilling to help themselves first. Are you willing to take the steps? Or, are you waiting for someone to do it for you?

Place your initials next to your answer.

_____ I am willing to take each of these steps in order to attain the life that I desire.

_____ I am NOT willing to take each of these steps in order to attain the life that I desire.

Choose wisely!

4 ESTABLISH WHY YOU MUST CHANGE

What are the drawbacks of where you are now?

A lot of us miss this important step. We forget to look at what is wrong with where we are now. We are told by motivational speakers and the like that we are supposed to find all of the good that we can in the world and focus solely on that. The truth is that we don't change unless there is enough pain in the situation that we are in and enough pleasure in the future that we desire. In Step 3, we discussed painting that picture of that ideal future that you are looking for. If you have a solid view of where you want to go, you must also have a solid view of where you DON'T want to be. Let's walk through how you do that.

"I don't like that I don't have the success that I am looking for. I don't like that I work 80 hours a week for no more money than I am getting. I don't like that I feel unappreciated. I don't like that I spend too much time doing the things in business that I don't enjoy." If you have said things like this, then you are not alone. You are a part of the group that realizes that there is more to life than what they are currently getting. The exercise that I would like for you to do now is to write out 10 things that you don't like about your current situation. What are the things that, if you stay the same, will end up costing you a great deal of your happiness?

1. _____

2. _____

3. _____

4. _____

5. _____

6. _____

7. _____

8. _____

9. _____

10. _____

Since your brain thinks in the present tense and more easily accepts this format as real, I want to get things in that same format to make them real. The goal is to build up some momentum towards the change that you are looking to achieve. If you were to look one year into the future and you did not take the action you wanted to in order to achieve success, what would that have cost you? Would it have cost you relationships? Would it have cost you financially? Would it have cost you emotionally, mentally, or physically? Everything that we do has a consequence. Every action has a result. This means that even when you make the choice to not do anything different, you are choosing a result. An example of what I am talking about would be...

"Today is December 1, 2015 and I have chosen not to pursue the goals that I had set. I have not gotten the education that I wanted. I have not put in the right effort to move my business forward. I have not learned the new things that I needed to learn in order to grow and develop. As a result of not doing what I knew that I needed to do, I now make less money than I did last year. My marriage is suffering because I am still unhappy with what I am doing and the results I am getting. I can't afford to take the vacations I want because I have not earned enough money. Every result that I am getting is a consequence of my choices. I do not blame anyone or anything else. I am responsible for my results."

Now it is your turn. Use the space below to write out the consequences and acceptance of responsibility for not taking action.

_____

_____

_____

_____

_____

_____

_____

_____

_____

If you are like me, even a little bit, then it hurts to write things like that. It hurts to take full responsibility for a lack of results. You are in control of you. You may not achieve all of your goals by taking action. You will achieve none of them, though, by not taking action. You need to see the pain in not exhibiting the right behaviors to move yourself and your business forward. We are motivated by the avoidance of pain and the pursuit of pleasure. That's it. If we know that those are the only two things that motivate us, then we need to build up as much decision-power as we can.

You are accountable. Whether you want to be or not, you are accountable. Accountability leads to consequences, good or bad. You are responsible for your results. If you don't like the results that you are getting, then exhibit different behaviors. You will not get new results if you don't do new things. Even though it can be painful, use that pain to drive you toward your goals. When I started in business, I operated partially out of the "Stark Raving Terror Of Poverty." This was a philosophy of remembering that I could decide to be broke, just the same as I could decide to be successful. Either result came from my choices. If I chose to not sell, build, and grow, then I chose to be in poverty. If I chose to bring in business, take care of clients, and expand my reach, then I chose to be successful. This principle applies to business, but it also applies to our personal relations. If we choose not to work on the things that make our relationships strong, then we are choosing to damage those relationships. People don't really "just grow apart." We stop trying to impress our spouse because "we already got 'em."

When you were dating, you spent hours working on ways to impress your potential mate. You took care of yourself, exercised, thought about what you were saying before you said it, etc. If you are not happy with your results in your relationship, ask yourself if your behaviors fit with someone who is "courting" another person. I want to point out that it does take two in any relationship to make it work. It generally starts with one person making the first move. Fair or not, if you want things to work in YOUR life, you have to be willing to make that move. You can use this exercise for any portion of your life for which you are unhappy with the current results. Never forget that the choice is yours and only yours.

5 DEFINE THE BENEFITS OF YOUR DESTINATION

William James was considered the father of American psychology. He defined the two human motivators as the **avoidance of pain** and the **pursuit of pleasure**. You have defined the pain associated with not pursuing your goals. Now, you must concentrate on the positive side of things and define the benefits of reaching your targets.

In Paulo Coelho's book, The Alchemist, Santiago is content to be a simple sheep herder until a dream of finding his treasure in the Egyptian Pyramids shakes him from complacency and puts a picture of what could be in front of him. Every time the boy begins to become complacent, the dream comes back. He learns to read the signs to know when to change direction, approach others, and move ever closer to his goal. One of the components of the book that really struck me was the fact that he had a picture of what he was supposed to achieve. He had a destination. For someone from Andalusia to end up in Egypt is more than chance. It is the relentless pursuit of a destination.

Think about something in your life that you wanted more than anything else that you could remember. Try to rekindle the fire in your belly that made you know, not think, but know that you had to pursue it. Your destination is your defining purpose in life. It is your masterpiece, by which you will be known or judged for all eternity. If you have but one masterpiece, and that masterpiece is your life, then it must be great!

Take a moment after this paragraph to picture what the destination will be like. Picture all of the benefits of achieving your heart's desire. I want you to breathe in the pleasing aromas around you, filling your lungs with the sweet smell of success. See your friends and loved ones smiling and laughing, as you entertain them and engage with them. You are in the home that you have earned. You are with the people who admire you and respect you. You are living the life that you know deep down in your soul was meant for you. Take just a few minutes right now to close your eyes and picture what perfection is like for you.

(Time to Visualize)

Every person on this earth was put here for a reason. Sadly, the majority of people will never realize that reason for existence. You, on the other hand, will be among the 2% who have a definite purpose, who know where they are going, and who know exactly what it will be like to be there. The universe moves to assist those who know exactly where they wish to go.

Take time to fill in the blanks with 20 benefits that you will receive once you have met your goals and reached your destination. Beside each of them, reinforce why that benefit is important or how it will make your life more pleasant, easier and better. It isn't important to put them in specific order. It is only important that you put each of them here and that you come up with all 20.

Benefit of Achieving   Why This
My Goal   Is Important

_____   _____

_____   _____

_____   _____

_____   _____

_____   _____

_____   _____

_____   _____

_____   _____

_____   _____

_____   _____

_____   _____

_____   _____

_____   _____

_____   _____

_____   _____

_____   _____

_____   _____

_____   _____

_____   _____

_____   _____

Your reason for existence is to fulfill your destiny on this earth. Your destiny on this earth is a reflection of the gifts that the Divine Creator put inside of you. You were made for greatness. Your destiny, your great desire, your destination is possible as long as you stack the odds in your favor. Your must be willing to fully participate here. Don't just skip through this. If you are reading this electronically, make a note with the note feature or pull out a note pad. If you are listening, then stop the audio and write out all 20 of these. This is very important.

It has been my experience over the last 15 years of working with people to become the best version of themselves and achieve their goals and dreams, that positive reinforcement is key. Any person that has full motivation will know what they are pursuing even more than they know what they are avoiding in life.

Take a moment to write out your statement of purpose below. You will need the following components individually in order to win.

1. What is your driving purpose or destination?

2. When will you arrive at that destination?

3. What will you give in order to achieve that destination?

4. Why will you always push forward and
    never give up?

By answering those four questions, you will be able
to articulate clearly what your life is all about and
move yourself in that right direction.

6 ACQUIRE THE RIGHT SKILLS AND KNOWLEDGE

Sir Francis Bacon said, "knowledge is power." I could not possibly agree more, with a small caveat. Knowledge is power when it is properly applied. Simply having the knowledge doesn't guarantee your success. You have to know what you are going to do with that knowledge and then take action to put it to good use.

"Wisdom is not a product of schooling but of the lifelong attempt to acquire it."
— Albert Einstein

The key to creating the right understanding of knowledge for you is that it is the pursuit of and acquisition of knowledge that will set you apart from your competitors. There are countless people in this world that believe that because they went to school for longer than you, they are smarter. The truth is that school is simply a platform for learning. You can learn in the library, online, in the coffee shop, or anywhere you fervently desire to add knowledge and skills to your life. There are several steps that you should follow in your pursuit of knowledge. When you follow these specific steps, the acquisition and application of knowledge are almost guaranteed.

Step 1: Discover the skills of the master.
When you look at the people who have already achieved what you want to achieve in life, you will begin to see patterns of things that they know. Look at the behaviors that they exhibit and see what their true strong points are. David Beckham, for example, was a brilliant soccer player who could kick the long shots and bend the ball in mid-air around his opponents. He had likely practiced that skill over and over and over again. Most people who are masters have studied their skill and have mastered a few very key aspects of the skill. It isn't so much that Mr. Beckham was the best at every position on the soccer field or even that he was incredibly versatile. He was a master at kicking the ball into the goal. Donald Trump seems to be better at making deals than any other business person around. He has not always been that good at assessing risk. He has always been masterful, however, at the art of the deal. Begin to look at the people in your industry or your chosen profession and discover the few things that they are better at

than anyone else. Your assignment for this section is to come up with three things that the best of the best do, related to what you want to do. If you want to be the best salesperson in the world and you know a salesperson that is better than you, then watch what they do. This will help you to see what skills they have and what skills you need to master. Keep it to the top three skills that they have. Write those out below...

1 _____

2 _____

3 _____

Notes: _____

Step 2: Outline three places that you can master those skills.

Each of us needs a place that we can learn something new. I have been teaching leadership and success principles for more than a decade and a half, yet I still go to seminars, read books, listen to audio programs, and pay a coach on a monthly basis. I am thankful that I learned a long time ago that I still had more to learn. In fact, the more I learn, the more I realize that I need to learn. I began wanting to be able to close deals easier when I made presentations, so I started looking at what the masters of persuasion knew and what they did.

People like Tony Robbins were very open about the fact that they took action in studying NLP (neuro-linguistic programming). So, I began looking at where I could learn the same skills that he was a master of. I found out that Richard Bandler and John Grinder were the creators of NLP and that it complimented theories such as the Attribution Theory that I had been teaching all along. I outlined organizations that taught the skills that I wanted to know and I chose a seminar to attend in Los Angeles. It was 5 days long and 12+ hours per day. It was intense. I found a series of books that were written by Bandler and some of his associates. I ordered and read those. I found an audio series that was put on by Igor Ledachowzki. I bought all of them and I listened to all of them, multiple times. I am a firm believer that you need multiple perspectives. You also need multiple exposures in order to master any skill.

When I was in college and studying literature, one of my professors told me that you could only consider yourself a master over a subject once you had read 100 books on it. I liked to read. I had trouble wrapping my mind around the number 100 at the time though. You would be amazed at how quickly you can conquer 100 books on success if success in your chosen area is your definite purpose in life. In the blanks below, write out the three things that you will attend, read, listen to, or participate in that will help you master the skills that you need.

1 _____

2 _____

3 _____

Notes: _____

Step 3: Go to all three of the places that you have
chosen and study the skills.

Don't sign up for a seminar and then Facebook
through the whole thing or check emails or be
distracted in any other way. As a society, we seem
to be so busy that we think we have to multi-task to
be happy. When you are learning, focus on
learning. When you are working, focus on working.
Don't spend your time running mentally from one
thing to the next. Your job is to make yourself as
successful as possible. That means that you must
acquire and implement new skills continuously. If
you are only half there, then you won't get even
half of what you need. I see people going to
seminars regularly who are there for the fellowship
instead of for the learning. Your objective at any
event should be to immerse yourself in what the
speaker/leader has to say, take notes, and jot down
how and when you will be able to apply what they
are teaching. Some people learn best by listening.
Some people learn best by writing notes. Some
people learn only when they go and implement what
they have learned. My recommendation to you,

based on what I have gleaned over the years on adult learning, is this… Listen intently if you are an auditory learner and then buy the audio program that accompanies the seminar. Most of them have one. Take notes feverishly if you are a kinetic learner. Then, go back and make more notes after the fact so that you ensure you have a plan of attack. Immerse yourself enthusiastically in the process, watching what everyone around you does and how they interact if you are a visual learner. Regardless of which of the three primary learning types you are, at the end of the day, every day, write out three important things that you learned. By doing this, you ensure that you are at least paying enough attention to get three items and you focus your brain on getting something each day from the process. The same premise applies to reading books, listening to audio programs, and even to being coached. If you are focused on getting something out of every experience, you will. If you are signing up for stuff to fulfill a requirement and you have no desire to learn, you won't. The choice is yours.

So, take a moment and write down 3 things that you have learned so far in this book that will help you to achieve more in life. It doesn't matter what they are. It just matters that you have three things.

1 _____

_____

2 _____

_____

3 _____

_____

Step 4: Put the skills and knowledge into practice.

As soon as you learn a new skill, you need to
employ that skill. I decided a while back that I
wanted to learn the skill of face reading. When I
am conducting workshops, coaching people, or
trying to sell something, it is extremely helpful to
know a little more about the person than they would
likely tell me. I read a book on face reading. I
bought a computer program that was interactive that
taught me about the facial features and structure. I
then attended a live event. I went to my three
places to learn. I then started reading people's faces
at parties, at church, at the coffee shop, etc. It was
fun and gave me the chance to practice on lots of
people for free. I would normally approach a
person that I didn't know or didn't know well and
ask them if they had ever had their face read before.
Pretty much everyone said no. I then asked
permission to read their face and tell them what I
saw. Most people were intrigued enough by the
concept that they were open to the idea. I didn't get
everything right. The first 5 or 6 times, I actually
got a lot of it wrong. I was even fumbling to flip

through my notes and through the book to make sense of some feature on their face. I kept implementing and kept implementing until I had mastered the art of face reading. In the first 60 days of wanting to master this skill, I read over 100 faces of people that I didn't know, and another 100 of people that I did know. The practice was great and it afforded me the opportunity to hone my skills.

Just like your muscles, any skill that you don't employ will atrophy. It will simply wither away. So, when you learn something, go do it! If you don't implement, you won't master. This is true of sales, speaking, soccer, face reading, or anything else that you wish to learn. Below, write out what you will do in the next 48 hours to implement a skill that you have been learning.

_____

_____

_____

_____

_____

Step 5: Get someone to coach you who can be brutally honest.

This is a tough one for most people. Mike Tyson used to have a guy that he paid to walk behind him and tell him how good he was. This man's only job was to let Mike know that Mike was the man. Don't get me wrong, I think Mike was the man. He was the undisputed man for a very long time. Mike also had a coach though. His coach didn't just tell him how awesome he was and how he didn't need to learn anything new. No, his coach was brutally honest about his jab, his cross, his upper cut, his foot work, his everything when it came to boxing. Often times, the best coach is not someone who is a master in the same arena as you. The reason this is true is that people who are masters struggle with describing why they are masters. A coach is designed to be an outside observer whose only desire is to help you succeed at a higher level. By laying your ego aside, you will be able to gain the right insight into what is holding you back and what can propel you forward. A coach can look at you and see through the smoke screen into what is really going on. Don't fool yourself and think that you have all the wisdom you need. There is always something more to learn.

Think about when super stars begin to fall. Movie stars, athletes, and those who seem to be larger than life were pushed to be their very best. When they stop listening to their coach and start listening only to the people who are telling them they are indestructible or above the law, that is when things come crashing down. I am all for surrounding yourself with positive people. I am even more for finding a person who will help you see every opportunity for growth, and capitalize on your strengths. That's what a great coach does. I want to encourage you to find a coach. In fact, find 2 or 3 that could coach you and interview them. Find the person that can push you the way you need to be pushed. An outside advisor makes for greater success.

Step 6: Find three more places to re-learn the skills and re-acquire the knowledge.

This is the same thing as the earlier paragraph. You aren't done because you learned from three people. Every time you master the skills of your trade at your given level, find three more people that are even better that you can learn from. Then, do it again!

Step 7: Put the skills and knowledge back into practice.

As soon as you master the new set of skills, go put those into practice over and over again until you are completely confident in your abilities. Then, demonstrate your abilities to your coach and see what she or he says about it.

Rinse, lather, repeat! Rinse, lather, repeat! You get the idea. The acquisition of knowledge is a never ending, high intensity, contact sport. Go get 'em!

7 PLAN YOUR ACTIONS

**"If you don't design your own life plan, chances are you'll fall into someone else's plan. And guess what they have planned for you? Not much."
--Jim Rohn**

One of the great challenges that I see in life is that people don't really plan out the specific actions they are going to take. People set goals on a regular basis and even map out targets for what they will acquire during the year. The problem isn't really with goal setting. In a book that I read recently, the author noted that more than 50% of people will give up on their New Year's resolutions before the end of January. By the time March hits, and we're ready for spring break, over 90% of people have given up on the goals they set just a couple of months earlier. We get too caught up in the idea that we need to map out the goals and the plans that we have on a grand basis. The truth of the matter is this... what you want to accomplish for the month is significantly less relevant than what you actually accomplish today. In this chapter, my goal is to help you establish what you need to do on a daily basis in order to accomplish what you wish to accomplish for the week, the month, the quarter, the year, and the rest of your life. By planning out the things that you will do on a daily basis, you prepare yourself the best for accomplishing great things. Let's take a look at what I mean by that. If your objective is to increase sales by 10% for your organization and you sold $1 million last year, that would mean that you need a $100,000 increase in sales. If each of your clients is worth approximately $50,000, then 20 clients are what make up your $1 million in sales. If you lose, on average, 10% of your client base each year, then you will need an extra two sales at $50,000 each on top of the increase in order to reach your goal. This means, that you need to take care of the 90% of the clients that you retain and add four new clients to your business. It takes you four presentations to close one new deal. It takes you five phone calls to set up one presentation. This means that you need to make 16 presentations throughout the year. It also means that you will need to make 80 phone calls during the year in order to accomplish your goal. If you make two phone calls per week, you should exceed your goals. My suggestion in planning your actions would be that you set aside one specific day each week that you make phone calls. You keep dialing until you get a chance to actually talk to the person who has the opportunity to tell you either yes or no. Let's say, for example, that you chose Tuesday's as your day for making phone calls. You would arrive at the office at 8:30 AM. You would get your coffee and turn on your computer and say hi to those that need a greeting. From 9 AM until 11 AM, you would have time blocked off for the calls. Within a two hour window, I would argue that you would be able to make those phone calls. By making the calls, you make your goals.

What we are not talking about here, is time management. There is a myth that you can manage your time. There is a reality that you can only manage what you put into your time. I want to deal with the reality and not with the myth. As you begin to look at how you manage the priorities of your day, most people will see that they waste an inordinate amount of time. They waste their time, giving up what they could accomplish by not focusing on the things that are important. A very simple process to map out what is most important to you, would be to outline the things that make the biggest difference in your day. I want you to take just a few minutes and write down the five most important things that you must do on a daily basis in order for you to be successful. Take a few minutes and do that now.

The five most important things that I must do on a

daily basis in order to be wildly successful are…

_____

_____

_____

_____

_____

Now, I want you to make a list of everything that you did in the last two days. It really isn't that critical that you remember every little thing. The point is to get you to see how many things that you actually did during the day. Take a few minutes and write those down now.

Everything that I can remember that I actually did in the last two days is as follows…

_____

_____

_____

_____

_____

_____

_____

_____

_____

_____

One of the most important things that you will learn in becoming successful is how to begin each day by performing the five critical behaviors before you do any of the other things on your list. It is extremely helpful to write out those five important things that you must do on a daily basis on a note card. Keep the note card where you can see it at your desk. Keep a copy of the note card in your vehicle. Then, ask yourself on a regular basis, "Am I doing the most important things that I must do in order to be successful?" I would go so far as to say that you should really map out every day the specific things that you're going to do and at the specific times you're going to do them. Remember, it is only the five things that you really need to map out. The rest of the things are not completely essential. If you don't get to those things, you can still be very successful.

Get A Calendar System

I do encourage you to use some type of calendar in order to help keep you on track. The type of calendar that you decide to use is less important than the fact that you have decided to use a calendar. You can use a notepad with the daily to do list. You can use a Franklin Covey Planner®. You can use a Google calendar or any other variation of a calendar system that fits you. You do, however, need to have some way of keeping track of what you're supposed to be doing next. The most successful people in the world have a plan. Their plan goes beyond attacking the problem in order to solve it. The plan really involves understanding what they are supposed to do, how they are supposed to do it, and when it's supposed to be done. I would encourage you to set actual goals for your life. In chapter 3, we talked about the five domains of life and where you would like to see yourself in five years. Now, you need to map out your goals for those five areas for the next one year. Do not set more than three goals per area. Any more than three and you will not keep up with them. It's okay to have only one goal per area. Each time that you set a goal, I want you to write out what you would have to do in order to accomplish that goal. Just like the example of increasing your revenue, you need to map out the specific things that will have to happen in order to accomplish the goal. You will then want to work backwards into the goal.

Reverse Engineering Success

In order to reverse engineer success, you map out the specific steps to succeeding at any given goal. You then want to map out how long it will take for each of those steps to be accomplished. Once you have mapped out the time it will take for each step, you want to work backwards from the date of success (one year from now). If a goal will take you 52 hours of effort for you to be successful at it, and you can only devote one hour per week to its accomplishment, then you will need 52 weeks in order to meet that goal. This means that you would need to start on the first week of January in order to be successful. Your assignment for this chapter is to map out your goals in each of the five domains of life and write out what it would take to meet each of those goals. Make sure that you map out the exact amount of time that would be needed for the goal to be accomplished. I would encourage you to map out each of the domains on a separate sheet of paper in a notepad. You're welcome to write them out or to type them up. The key is that they need to be written out in one way or another. This assignment will likely take you longer than some of the others. Your life and your future are important enough for you to invest the time in this.

I am excited as I visualize the success that you are already creating in your life. I think of the things that you are accomplishing now and the feeling of success that accompanies that. As you set your goals, think about the following.

It's not the number of times that we get knocked down in life that will matter. It is the fact that we get up one more time than we got knocked down that ultimately makes us a success.

The Five Domains of Life to Set Goals and Actions for are:

Personal Relationships

Goal 1: _____

Goal 2: _____

Goal 3: _____

Financial Life

Goal 1: _____

Goal 2: _____

Goal 3: _____

Physical Life

Goal 1: _____

Goal 2: _____

Goal 3: _____

Spiritual Life

Goal 1: _____

Goal 2: _____

Goal 3: _____

Psychological & Emotional Life

Goal 1: _____

Goal 2: _____

Goal 3: _____

•

8 FAIL FORWARD

The word fail originated in the 13th Century and meant to be deficient in or lacking something. It very quickly became associated with sin, as in to fail God or the church. The negative connotation of failing at something goes way back and is generally seen as something that ends a direction. Think back to some of the things in your life that have been considered failures. How did those failures effect you and the direction that you were going in life? How did failing stop you? How did failing redirect you? What is interesting to me is the number of complete and total failures in this world that were wildly successful as a result of failing, but not stopping.

Let's take a look at two profiles of failures that helped to shape the world that we live in and map out what their failure did for the world. By studying people who have failed their way to the top, I believe that you will begin to see the same pattern that I have seen. I believe that you will begin to see that it isn't the failure that is the problem. In fact, I have seen that it is the failure that is required to teach people who they really are and how they can find their true purpose in life.

Thomas Alva Edison was, by the definition of almost anyone around, a tremendous success in life. If you would have been around during his early years, however, you might have seen in him what many adults saw in him. Edison was the youngest of 7 children. From the beginning, he had a curious mind, but also a wandering mind. When he began his "official schooling," his instructor, the Reverend Engle, was frustrated with him because of his "wandering" mind. Edison would think of what he wanted to think of instead of what the instructor wanted him to think of. After only three months of schooling, it was clear to Reverend Engle that Edison was a failure at formal education. His education in the traditional process ended at that point. He never returned to school. Edison's mom, Nancy Matthews Elliott, took over at that point. She encouraged his creativity and his drive to learn new things in his own way. Edison's first failure was at conforming to the educational path of the rest of the world. Thank goodness for that failure because it led to him unlocking the mysteries of the world with the creativity of his own mind and spirit. Much of Edison's education at home came from reading R.G. Parker's <u>School of Natural Philosophy</u> and <u>The Copper Union.</u> His true success stemmed from his mother's belief that he had something incredible to live for and that he would help to change the world. It is fascinating to me how many great leaders were the creation of their mom's belief in them when they were young. When we develop a self-belief in our children, based on them working hard and discovering new things, they can accomplish virtually anything. Edison was not coddled by his mother, or his father, but he was encouraged by both. He had an incredible drive to work hard. When that was coupled with his ingenious curiosity, it made for a rather remarkable young man.

Edison began working as a young boy. He would sell candy and newspapers on the train as he rode back and forth from Port Huron to Detroit, Michigan. He had set up his own portable lab in one of the back cars of the train to conduct experiments when he was not in "sales mode." His study and experiments with both qualitative analysis and chemical processes was put to an end when he had an accident on the train with his lab and caught the rail car on fire. This failure led to him taking a new direction in life. He was still just a boy, but he knew that he needed to have a more stable environment for his experiments. The conductor of the train boxed his ears when his experiment caused the fire. In one account, Edison indicates that this was the cause of hearing loss that he suffered. He did tell the story in a few different ways over the years, explaining his hearing loss. Failing at the candy and newspaper sales on the train because of the experiment led to him focusing on more solid ground.

Edison began selling newspapers on the street. He had liked the exclusivity that he had on the train and used that same model on the street. He obtained the exclusive rights to sell newspapers on the road. He also began typesetting and publishing a paper. This gave him greater profits and greater control over the paper. He opened locations and had others sell for him in order to make a piece of the profits. He had a significant number of shops in that first year. Failing at the train car sales model led him to learn how to leverage the efforts of others. Eventually, Edison would found 14 companies throughout his life. In selling the newspapers on the road, one young lady that worked in one of his shops caught his eye. Mary Stilwell was one of his employees at 16 years old. Two months after meeting Miss Stillwell, Edison and Stilwell were married. Not only did Edison discover how to be an entrepreneur, he also discovered the woman he was to marry as a result of leaving the train car, candy selling business.

Edison followed this same pattern with every failure that happened in his life. When something didn't work, he simply picked himself up and looked to the next thing. Each failure held within it the next opportunity. Napoleon Hill, who studied Edison and his life, learned that "The seed of equivalent benefit always resides in what man would call failure." In an interview where Edison was asked why he kept going when he had failed 10,000 times to create the electric light bulb, he replied, "I never failed; I just discovered 10,000 ways not to create the electric light bulb." His incredible ability to fail forward lead to him being known as "The Wizard of Menlo Park." He leveraged and cultivated the talents of others. He never believed that failure was the end. He simply believed that failure was the foundation for the creative spark that would lead to the next better thing.

Steve Jobs, one of the founders of Apple Computers, is another example of what it means to fail your way to the top. Jobs was given up for adoption by his biological mother, who was a graduate student at the time. His biological father was also a graduate student. The one condition that his mother had when she gave him up was that he had to be adopted by an educated family who would send him to college. The original adoptive family fell through and Jobs was adopted by Paul Job's family. Paul was not educated, but he was very good as a mechanic. Jobs was incredibly curious and thought through things differently than most people that he was around. He loved the idea of creating something that would last. When he first went to college, he attempted to fit into the educational norms. It just didn't work. He would figure out quickly that he was going to fail at traditional education. His first "failure" was that he dropped out of school. His parents were working extremely hard to put him through school and he really wasn't into learning the way the professors wanted to teach. Because of this realization, Steve dropped out. This led to him wandering, traveling, and trying to discover who he was as a person. He lived as a hippy for a number of years. He found a way to travel to India because he wanted to learn how to be enlightened. Almost dying on that trip, he discovered who he really was. In his early 20's, he met an incredible engineer name Steve Wozniak. Woz loved to create circuit boards and was very into computers. Jobs knew how to take the creations of others and make them marketable. It wasn't long before Jobs and Woz would decide to form a computer together in California. They found a way to raise capital and brought on a third partner, and thus Apple Computers was born. They had their share of ups and downs, but the big failure in Steve Jobs' life was when John Sculley out-maneuvered him in the board room and ended up getting Steve Jobs fired from his own company. Jobs was angry about the incident. Although it definitely shaped the moves that he made going forward, he did his best to not let that define him. Instead, he began looking around for what to do next. "Next Computers" was his venture. This was a small company that was designing an operating system that needed funding. Jobs was just the man for the adventure. Along with Next, Jobs also purchased Pixar, who made animation computers and software. Jobs worked a deal to sell the computers to Disney and eventually leveraged that deal to be a partner with Disney in the movie business. Pixar changed the face of movie animation with "Toy Story" and 10 blockbuster hits that followed. Next ended up being bought by Apple for 400 Million Dollars! And, Steve Jobs was asked to come back and run Apple after it had declined significantly under John Sculley's leadership. Jobs came back to Apple as the CEO, after much coaxing, but he did so with no salary and no stock options. He wanted to prove the point that he was there for the company and not for the money. Jobs failed several times at business, but ended up succeeding because he never quit. He learned something from each and every failure. Because he learned a lesson, he propelled himself forward.

When you look at people and the failures that they experience, you see some common traits.

1. Successful people see failure as an event. When you see failure as an event, you simply brush yourself off and move forward. When you see failure as a person, as you, then you crumble and feel sorry for yourself. Failure is simply an event. It is often the exact catalyst that is needed to move you to the next level.
2. Something inside of the greats has to get out. There is an art that lives inside

of inventors, painters, writers, and entrepreneurs that has to get out. Edison had to invent. Jobs had to start and build companies. Van Gogh had to paint. Each person has an expression of themselves that wants to get out. The greats will give it an outlet and they will succeed because of it.

3. One more time is the mantra of people who will succeed in life. They know that they must try one more time, even when trying again seems very painful. Every time they get knocked down, they get up, brush themselves off, and try one more time.

4. Do the work! Successful people are absolutely NOT lazy. They believe in hard work. They show up every day and express their creativity. They know that they have to do the work in order to get the results. They don't wait on the world to make them successful. They make themselves that way by working hard.

9 FOCUS YOUR ACTIONS

Beliefs – Thoughts – Attitudes – Behaviors – Results

When I was 9 years old, I was allowed to start Martial Arts. I had seen the other students, mostly kids, in the basement of the library, learning to kick and punch. I was fascinated, mostly because of how scrawny of a kid I was, with the idea of being able to actually defend myself against bullies. Like most small towns, we had several bullies that were relentless to the other kids. And, like most small towns, the teachers didn't really do anything about it. I guess they figured it was a "right of passage." Up until that point, I had begun to believe that I somehow deserved to be picked on and pushed around. I never liked being bullied. I don't think anyone does. I decided that I needed to figure things out, though. I wasn't going to sit around my whole life and feel like I deserved for bad things to happen to me. Once I joined, I was hooked. I was hooked because the lessons that I was learning in Martial Arts were more than just kicking and punching. They were about how to live life the right way. They were lessons on controlling my beliefs. Just like the tree below, it is what is beneath the surface that has the greatest impact on the life of the organism.

It is a person's root beliefs that will establish the path upwards that they follow. What people see is the fruit, the leaves, the branches, and the trunk.

If the tree doesn't have a healthy root system, though, it won't matter what the top looks like. It will decay and die soon. The truth about life is that we are a representation of our core beliefs. What we believe, particularly about ourselves, will determine what the world sees. The world will see what we actually see in ourselves. It is this image of self that creates the world around us. Think about a person that only sees bad in the world. They continuously think that others are out to get them, or cheat them. What happens to them regularly? That's right, they get cheated and the world ends up bad. Their roots are searching for cheater nutrients. And guess what, those roots will search as hard as they need to in order to find the negativity that they seek. We must learn to control the beliefs that exist inside of us, at our core, in order to control the outcomes that we achieve.

I once believed that boards could not be broken with my hand. I had been in martial arts for only a few months when my instructor brought a bunch of 1 by 10 boards to class. He set up a couple of cinder blocks and demonstrated how easy it was to break through a board with his hand. It looked incredibly easy when he did it. The problem was, I still believed that the board could stop my hand. So, when I first tried to break the board, I hit it as hard as I could and it seemed to hit back. My hand stopped at the board and bounced back with a brand new throbbing sensation. I did NOT break the board. My instructor carefully explained the principle of breaking again to me and to the other

dozen or so kids that were rubbing their hands now.
I will never forget the lesson. Sang Ju Cho
explained...

*The problem that each of you is having is that
you do not believe that you can break through
the board. You are focusing on the board itself
and you are hitting the board. You should
never hit the board when you wish to break
through the board. You should hit the target on
the other side of the board. Once you believe
that the board has no power to slow you down
from your target, then your boards will break
to get out of your way. Now, choose a target at
least 6 inches past your board and allow the
board to not exist.*

I was almost in shock as to how easy it was to
break a board when the board no longer presented
itself as a barrier in my mind. On my very next try,
I punched through the board as if it did not exist.
The lesson that I learned was that I needed to adjust
my focus. My beliefs, up to that point, indicated
that punching a board would result in my hand
hurting and the board not breaking. My new belief
was that I could focus past the board and believe
that the board no longer presented a problem for
me. The second that I changed my belief, the
problem went away.

Think about the things that you believe about
business, about success, about money, about life.
Some of the things that I learned when I was young
have been the most damaging. Well meaning

adults, often parents, will say things that influence us to think the wrong thoughts. They will say things like, "All rich people are crooks." They will say things like, "Money is the root of all evil." They will say, "It isn't worth giving up your life to be successful." I am sure that they mean well when they say these things, but it is their beliefs that they are pushing. They don't have to be yours. When you examine the origin of these phrases, you get a different picture of what the world actually is. For example, I used to hear my father use the bible verse, "It is easier for a camel to pass through the eye of a needle than a rich man to get to heaven." It wasn't until I began exploring the origins of these phrases that I realized how screwed up the belief was. In the original biblical text, it said that "It is easier for a camel to enter the gates of a city than it is for a rich man to get to heaven." For a camel to enter the gates of a city, its owner had to remove the cargo from its back and the camel had to crawl into the gate on its knees. This was not impossible, but it required focus and the removal of stuff. In the text that says that "Money is the root of all evil," the word money was originally "mammon." Mammon means stuff, possessions, or belongings. The original text also says, "The love of mammon before the love of God is the pathway to all kinds of evil." In other words, it isn't having stuff, or money, that makes a person bad. It is making the money and the stuff more important than their relationship with God. The last phrase that really gave me problems was, "It is better to give than to receive." When I began exploring that phrase, I came across its origin as being, "It is better to be in a position to give than in a position to need." Wow is all I can think on this one. This reverses the meaning. It now means that it is better to be in a position of wealth and success so that you are able to help than it is to be in a position of lack or wanting so that you need help.

I have found, when I looked around openly, that there are a tremendous number of generous and helpful rich people in this world. There is example after example of how people became wildly successful and then made the world into a better place. There are three levels of focusing your mind that you must take into account in order to find the success that you desire.

1. You must focus your self-talk. The things that you say to yourself when you are the only one listening are critical. When you focus on the things that you have done wrong, you will find that you do more and more things wrong. When you focus on the things that you accomplish each day, you will do more and more things right. This takes a little discipline, and some consistent practice. When you mess something up, instead of telling yourself that you are "such a screw-up," it is much better to describe how much smarter you are now that you have learned a new lesson. When something goes wrong, ask yourself what lesson you have learned, then focus on the increased wisdom that you now possess. Only allow

yourself to say good things to you. Talk to yourself as a winner! Talk to yourself as the kind of person that makes great things happen! Tell yourself every day about the gifts that you possess. This self-talk will set the wheels in motion to help you believe what you need to believe in order to succeed.

2. You must focus your success beliefs. If you don't like people with money, you will never be a person with money! If you don't like, or look down on, people who have achieved great things, then you will never be one of those people. You can never have what you disdain. When you look at a person who has millions and think, "I can't stand people who run around doing whatever they want with their money," you are putting a nail in your own coffin and preventing yourself from ever attaining what they have attained. You have to look at people and see the good in them. When a person has money, they have created the right belief about money. If you don't believe that you deserve money, then you may earn a lot, but you will lose it. A great book on understanding your money blueprint is Secrets of The Millionaire Mind, by T. Harv Ecker. Ecker says that everyone has a money blueprint. He says that your beliefs will create your world. I believe it! I learned at 9 years old that I needed to control my beliefs in order to break through

barriers. I would encourage you to write out what you think are your limiting beliefs. Write them out and then write a new belief in its place that would not limit your success. There is a place for this at the end of this chapter.

3. You must focus your attitude. Your attitude is just like your clothes. Every day, you get up and put on your new set of clothes. If you put on your old clothes each day, you will start to smell bad pretty quick. By day 3 or day 4, your friends will start to notice the stench and they will shy away from you. If you don't wake up every day and decide on the right attitude, you will find that your attitude stinks within a few days, just like your clothes would. You have a choice about your attitude. A quick fix that will help with your attitude is to wake up and smile for at least 2 minutes straight first thing in the morning. When you choose to smile, you will find that your attitude refreshes itself. The physiological act of looking happy is the quickest way to make yourself actually feel happy. Happiness alone doesn't make you a success. However, happiness with a positive attitude is one of the most important ingredients for success. If you have a positive attitude, you will get up and try another time. You will believe that good is possible and success is within your reach. If you are negative, you believe that all is lost and there is no hope of

success. The choice is yours. Choose
wisely! Your livelihood depends on you
choosing a good attitude.

Now that you believe the right things, you will
need to look at one more aspect of your focus. You
need to look at what you allow into your time.
That's right, it isn't about managing your time. It is
about what you allow into your time. Time is finite,
or limited. What you make into a priority in your
life is what is within your control, not time itself.
So, a very simple exercise to determine what will
get you the success you desire is to look at what you
allow into your time and choose what matters most.
In my book, Just Make Time, I talk about the Pareto
Principle. This principle indicates that 20% of the
things that we do bring us 80% of our results. The
key is to identify those things in the 20% category
and do them before we do anything else each day.
On the list below, you can list up to 5 things that
have the greatest impact on you being successful in
your endeavors on the left hand side, and as many
as you would like on the right. The right hand side
of the chart is for everything you do during a day,
other than the 5 or fewer most important things. Go
ahead and fill in the chart below.

Most Important To My Success	Everything Else That I Do During A Day

If you are like most people, it is a little difficult to narrow the most important things down to only 5. However, when you truly look at what brings you success, you find that there are really less than 5 things that are critical every day. They key to focused success is to always start on the left! Don't do the things on the right until you have done the things on the left first. If you will examine your beliefs, the roots of who you are, and intentionally create the right beliefs, you will find success. You are the master of your destiny! You are in control of where your life goes. You simply have to decide to look past the problems and focus on a point of success that you will hit. The moment you decide to focus on your success, you will begin to see a difference in your life. The problems that arise will simply be bumps in the road instead of brick walls that you run into. The last part of this chapter is the area for you to write out what beliefs are limiting you and what you could rewrite your beliefs to be in order to make them positive.

Limiting Belief: _____

_____

_____

New Belief: _____

_____

_____

Limiting Belief: _____

_____

_____

New Belief: _____

_____

_____

Limiting Belief: _____

_____

_____

New Belief: _____

_____

_____

Limiting Belief: _____

_____

_____

New Belief: _____

_____

_____

Limiting Belief: _____

_____

_____

New Belief: _____

_____

_____

When you define your beliefs, you are defining your thoughts. When you define your thoughts, you are defining your attitudes. When you define your attitudes, you are defining your actions. When you define your actions, you are defining your results. Everything begins with having the right beliefs!

10 BUILD A FOLLOWING

You will never get yourself or your organization to the place it should be by doing it all alone. You will need to find people who can understand what you are doing and who will get behind your idea. You are looking for people who truly want to connect with you and where you are going. Pushing people, tricking people, or manipulating people will eventually catch up to you and will end very, very badly. Having a following indicates that people DESIRE to follow you because you are leading them. To be a great leader, you must be "other-centered."

There are three key components to building a following. By following these three components, or key acts, you will have the greatest likelihood of others helping to propel you to the success that you desire. These components are…

1. Create change that is good for other people, not just for you.
2. Be a motivational educator.
3. Live as if you are already succeeding.

By focusing your efforts in these three ways, you will find that other people will go out of their way to be a part of where you are going. Before we get too far into this, however, it is important to understand how some other people are attempting to build their followings.

There are a number of larger brands who are attempting to use mass-hypnosis to create their following. They are attempting to push their ideas out to the masses and find ways to bypass their conscious mind and implant their ideas in the subconscious. Think about the last couple of drug commercials that you have seen from big pharmaceutical companies. The way in which they accentuate the positive of their drug using specific tonalities and images of people who are happy and then change their tone for the negatives, while still presenting happy images, is a form of hypnotic communication. Even though they readily admit that their drug may cause death, dismemberment, loose bowels, low libido, dry mouth, blurry vision, slurred speech, random howling sounds, sweaty palms, bad breath, crossed eyes, and loss of various limbs, they do get you to focus on the fact that you will likely have clearer skin. These companies, with the help of great writers and visual imagery, have found a way to get you to see what they want you to see about them and to avoid what they want you to avoid. Beer commercials show scantly dressed models having fun and connecting with great friends. They indicate that life is a party and that if you just drink their beer, you will be skinny, beautiful, have lots of friends, and never feel alone again. They do this through hypnotic suggestion. Vodka print ads are incredibly good at hiding images of naked women in their ice cubes. They are tapping into the easier to persuade portion of your brain in the hopes of getting you to turn loose of your cash. I will have to say… they are pretty good at it too. The problem with this path is two-fold. First, it takes a lot of money to push your persuasive message into enough subconscious minds to make a real difference. People need to see this image 10 or more times. It used to be that people only needed to see it a few times to be persuaded, but we are so overloaded with this imagery that we are becoming more and more desensitized to its effects. Second, this type of advertising is still a manipulation. It doesn't offer any truth or leadership. It simply offers an alternate reality that doesn't normally exist. At some point, people will figure out that having clearer skin, but no left arm, was a pretty bad trade. They will see that drinking that six pack a day does not, in fact, provide them with a six-pack set of abs. They will then have to make a different decision as to why they are using your product or service. It is very possible that they will resent you at this point, while still using your product.

It isn't your goal to simply have a better mousetrap than your competition. The goal should be to have people that truly believe in you and your company and want to see you succeed. You are looking for an evangelical belief in where you are going because you have provided real and lasting value. This brings us to the first component of your success. You are trying to provide change that makes a person's life actually better. I once met the guy that invented the little plastic strips that hang off of the shelves in the front of Wal Mart, and most grocery stores. These strips of plastic are used to hang chips, candy, and other impulse purchases right beside the registers. It is a relatively simple concept that he came up with, but it significantly impacted the bottom line of the stores that used them. These are high-profit items that people will buy because they are in front of them. The stores benefited greatly from buying these plastic strips from the inventor. They told their friends in other stores about how much they had helped. They ordered extra, just to have them on hand. They talked at conferences about the benefits of this product. This product was good for them. It helped them to run their businesses more efficiently and to make a better profit. I have yet to see an advertisement for little plastic strips that hang off of a shelf and create impulse purchase opportunities. I haven't needed to see a commercial. The product is good for the stores, so the stores did the advertising for the inventor. He had to hustle and show people how the product worked in the beginning. Because he was willing to talk to people and demonstrate how the product would benefit them, they are now going out of their way to bring him business. It took one Wal Mart manager wanting to purchase the item in a small West Texas town to tip the scales. With that purchase, Wal Mart saw the benefit and bought them for all, yes all, of their stores. They continue to buy these strips and the success of his product continues to flourish because people believe in him and his little plastic strips. He continues to look for ways to make life better for others. He doesn't think about the money or what is good for him. He thinks about what is good for the people that he serves. This makes him a great industry leader, and it makes him a successful one as well.

The second aspect of building a following is to be a motivational educator. Think about the companies that you enjoy doing business with. Think about the feeling that you have when you purchase from your favorite company. Don't you feel excited about the purchase? Don't you buy from people that you believe know what they are talking about? Doesn't it frustrate you to go to a store and ask a technical question about a product, just to realize in the first sentence of the employee's response, that they have no clue what they are talking about. I have found myself doing a little research on a product, just enough to be dangerous, and then going to several stores to see who knew the right answer to my question. This is a test that I like to do. I want to know who has done their homework and who can actually help me. An example of this would be just before Christmas, when I began asking questions about new TV's. I researched what the difference between a Smart TV and a regular TV was and then made my way to the stores. Only one person at one store could tell me what the actual difference was. The rest of them made up answers that didn't sound real, even if I hadn't known the answer going into the conversation. When I worked in retail, I spent any downtime reading about the difference between the products that I sold. Yes, I was the guy who read the technical manuals. I also kept track of what people said about the products after they bought them. This way, I had something worthwhile to offer my customers. I was excited about the things that I was learning and I was excited about having something more to offer my customers each day. In order to be an educator, you have to be educated. You have to take time to learn what your products or services can do for the customer or client. You have to know what the competition has to offer. Once you master the information, you keep learning and growing. You are never done learning what you need to know. Once you master the information, you practice the delivery of the information. You pay careful attention to your body language, your tone, and your overall presentation. If you do this, you begin to be the "go-to" person for information. People will spend more money with you if they believe you know more than they do. You need to be equipped with information and charm in order to inspire others to want to follow your advice. If you consistently give advice that is good for the customer, then you will be trusted by the customer and their friends. If you are excited while you are giving this great advice, then you will find that your customers, their friends, and the friends of their friends will go out of their way to say great things about you and show their pride in purchasing from you.

The third component of building a following is to live as if you are already succeeding. This is not to say that you should go out and buy a sports car and spend money like you were already rich. This component deals with treating customers like a successful person would treat them. Think about a person that you know that is wildly successful in their chosen field. Think about what successful people do in taking care of their customers. Think about the behavioral patterns, and the beliefs of successful people. To live as if you are already succeeding means that you exhibit the same behaviors as a successful person would exhibit. It means that you model greatness. The reason that someone else is more successful than you are is that they are doing the things that are necessary for success and you are not. Some people say, "but their definition of success is different than mine." I never said to look at someone that is richer than you are. I said to look at a person that is more successful. Use your definition of success. Find that person, or those people, that are accomplishing what you wish to accomplish and then model their behaviors and their beliefs. If you will do this, you will begin to achieve the same results that they have achieved. Everything in life is simply cause and effect. If you exhibit the right behaviors (cause), you will get the right results (effect). Act as if you are a successful person by putting in the efforts and exhibiting the beliefs and behaviors that successful people exhibit.

Building a following is about connecting with people. It is about creating a reason for others to desire to have a relationship with you and/or your organization. Regardless of the size of the organization, everything really is still about connecting!

11 ESTABLISH YOUR EXIT STRATEGY

Within the first several years of being in business, each business owner will need to decide whether their strategy is to sell the business to someone else or to sell it to themselves. When a person goes into business, they often don't think about how they are going to finish things off. Instead, they think about what they are going to do to get things started. If you are only thinking of 1 move at a time, you are not thinking strategically. Entrepreneurial ventures are like an incredible game of chess. If you are ever to be a chess-master, you have to be able to think not just one or two moves ahead, but through all of the moves and counter-moves. You have to be able to see the cause-effect relationship of each action that you take. By thinking through every step, you position yourself to think contingently. There are actually four places to sell your business. They are...

1. Sell the company to a person who buys and runs businesses. The harsh truth of the matter is that many entrepreneurs are good at the start, but they fizzle out in the stretch. Business, when it is successful, can be a grind. It is getting up every day and doing the things that are most important for the success of the business that day. It is remembering to do your accounting, file your taxes, pay the rent, and do every other detail necessary for your success. There are people who are truly cut out to run companies, but they are not cut out to start them. You may be the starter, but not the finisher. There isn't any shame in that. In fact, there are lots of people who have gotten very rich from starting a company and taking it past the proof of concept, and then flipping it to the distance runner. Just like flipping houses, you can flip your ideas into some incredible cash. You will want to identify if you are the type of person who does very well with the creativity and innovation, but doesn't fare so well with the maintenance of all things standardized.
2. Sell the company to investors (go public).

Andrew Carnegie, despite his open disdain for Wall Street, ended up rolling all of his enterprises together and selling them off to a group of investors. Charles Schwab, who really made a name for himself in this transaction, put the deal together. In that sales move, he sold his companies, as a conglomerate, for $400 million. This was an extremely significant sum in the early 1900's. This is a significant sum today as well. Taking a company public is no small feat, but it has been systemized to the point that it can be done, if you are willing to work at it. To take a company public, a person can make an incredible amount of money, or value, for themselves in a single day. Once a company is public, it is subject to significantly more scrutiny than a privately held corporation. If this is the path that you see for your organization, then publicity and partnerships are critical. You need the right accounting firm to represent you in preparing your financials. Everything must be extremely clean. You also need to obtain as much press as possible about what you are doing and the benefits of your organization to the world. If you can enlist the support of one or more of the big financial institutions, your share prices will rise and your value with grow exponentially. This seems to be the goal of many budding companies. Just be sure that you enlist the people who have already been to where you want to go. Expertise is critical with this path.

3. Sell the company to yourself. You are deciding that this is what you want to do for the rest of your life. In reality, many people start this way without realizing it. This is what can be referred to as buying a job if you are the practitioner type. There are really two possibilities for how you sell yourself on the idea of keeping the company. You can either intend to be in the mix, as the expert, for the rest of the time that you can work, or you can own the company and hire talented people to run it for you. Either way, it is the decision to keep it that matters. If you have built a company that runs without you in the middle of it, and it is producing significant revenues for you, there may be very little reason to ever get rid of it. If it is your cash machine, don't turn it off. Don't kill the "goose that lays the golden eggs." Owning a profitable company is an incredibly satisfying experience.

4. Sell the opportunity inside of the company to your employees. Many entrepreneurs that wish to remain connected, but are uneasy with turning over total control, will choose to bring up key employees as partial owners. This is generally done in the form of stock bonuses for performance, or the sale of stock to employees. When the business owner sells off stock to existing employees, it can

be a great way to give others the opportunity for ownership success, and a way to sell to someone that might not be able to buy otherwise. For service businesses, this is a great opportunity. It is difficult to sell a service business because of the need to transfer trust. When a service business, such as an accounting firm, or a training company, gets sold to a stranger, it is very likely that much of the business will simply go away. When an employee is transitioned in to the ownership seat over a period of five years, clients become familiar with the up-and-comer, and transfer their attachment to the new owner. As the new owner engages more and more with the customer base, the owner simply begins stepping out of the spotlight. Generally, the new owner will make payments, out of the revenues of the company, for a set timeframe or amount, until the company is considered purchased. There is a higher level of risk of the new owner not doing what they are supposed to, but it allows you to circumvent the banks and generally gets you more money than you would have gotten on a straight sale.

Your exit strategy should be planned out as soon as possible. The ideal situation would be for you to actually map out the markers in your business plan that would indicate which direction should be followed. You can map out multiple possibilities, and possibly even some that are not listed here.

Think of it like creating "if-then" statements. If this happens, then this will be the direction that we take. There are several resources printed in this chapter that will help you to map out your decision as to what direction is best for you.

12 NEVER LET ANYONE STAND IN YOUR WAY

The reality in which you choose to exist is the reality in which you must live. The harsh truth that you face is that you are the one who creates your reality. You are exactly who and where you have chosen to be. If someone is in your way, it is because you have given them permission to be there. The following story should help you understand that it is your choice to succeed With Or Without Someone Else.

Shane's story

Shane was 34 years old and had been in business for himself since he was 24. This was his 11th year to focus on finding his dream. Over the last decade, Shane had finished out each year with about the same result as every other year before that. His first year in business was a struggle, but he made it. His second year in business was really pretty good. He made $100,000 and did right at $200,000 in revenue. His third year, he did $300,000+ in revenue and still made $100,000. His fourth year, and every year after that, he did between $350,000 and $400,000 in revenue and made right at $100,000. Regardless of how much revenue he generated, he seemed to end up making $100,000. He couldn't figure out why he was stuck at this level and why he couldn't move past it. This has been his struggle for a solid decade. When Shane and I met, his objective was to figure out how to move past this plateau and make more for himself and his family. He wanted to figure out what the challenge really was. As he began talking about his history, his beliefs, and his challenges, it became clear that there were several people that were actually in his way. The first person that was holding him back was himself. He did not see himself as the kind of person that could make $250,000 or $500,000 or even more in revenue. If you are like Shane and can't see yourself at the next level, then you are in your own way mentally. To begin his transformation, I had him begin to visualize himself making $1,000,000 per year in personal income and billing twice that in his business. He was to spend 10 minutes per day seeing himself already at that level. Second, he explained to me that his banker would not loan him the capital that he needed to buy more equipment and he did not make enough money to buy the extra equipment without the loan. His focus had rested on the "no" that he had gotten at the bank. He felt that the support of his banker was required to be successful at the next level. I used the problem solving process with him to get him to understand what his options really were. He had jumped from the problem to the singular solution and therefore the rejection. He had not defined his need. He had defined his problem. No matter what the challenge is, there is a solution. Very seldom is the solution simple and obvious. If it were, the problem would already be gone. The following are the six steps that I walked Shane through in order to realize that he could succeed With Or Without Someone Else.

1. Define the Need: Don't define what is stopping you and what you can't overcome. Instead, define the need that you have. When you focus on the need, you focus on how you will get there. When you focus on the problem, you tend to focus on why you haven't gotten there. Don't dwell on your excuses. Instead, focus on where you need to go and why you need to go there.

2. Brainstorm for Options: When you brainstorm, there is no evaluation of the ideas that are generated. It is ideal to set a specific amount of time, usually 5 to 10 minutes, that you will come up with as many ideas as possible to meet the need that you have. During this phase, any idea is a good one. I even brought in a few outside entrepreneurs to generate ideas. This is often the hardest part for people who are

stuck in a rut. They want to focus on what won't work and so do other people. Don't let negativity get in your way, whether it is from you or from someone else. Write down every idea. I had to reiterate the rules for this step several times with Shane, as well as with the other entrepreneurs. It can be difficult to suspend judgment, but it is liberating when you do.

3. Evaluate your Options: During this phase, you will go back through all of the ideas that you brainstormed and measure them against the following criteria...

   a. Is it legal? If it is illegal or could possibly be illegal, don't do it. You don't want to risk this. If you get put in jail, you will have more than other people in your way, you will have bars in your way.

   b. Is it moral/ethical? Don't do anything that is seen as or is clearly immoral or unethical. Your reputation is what you have. As an entrepreneur, your reputation is everything.

   c. Is it possible? You have to measure whether or not it is possible for you to accomplish it with the resources that you have. You need to identify whether you have the resources, the skills, and aptitudes to accomplish the idea.

4. Choose your Plan: At this point, you are choosing which idea or group of ideas will

be the very best moving forward. The key to choosing a plan is in the commitment that comes from the decision. To me, making a decision means eliminating the "non-options." When you strip away the inessentials, you are left with the possibilities that will actually work. Choosing the plan of action means stripping away what won't work and assigning specific roles to people. When a role is assigned, deadlines are attached as well.

5. Implement your Plan: It's now time to take the ideas that you believe will be the best and put them into play. You should have a timeline of events or measurables that will happen and who will be responsible for each of them. Each person should have clear instructions and should take action now to make something happen. Within 24 hours of the assignment, you want each of the participants to have done something to move things forward. Keep things flowing until they are completed!

6. Evaluate: This step is critically important. In our organization, we actually do this step before and after the implementation phase. Before we implement, we will do a "pre-mortem" that outlines all of the things that we can assume could go wrong. We then create contingency plans to deal with the issues. After we have implemented, we do a "post-mortem" on the project. We look at what went right and what went wrong. We

look at the part that each of us played in the
steps and then outline what we would do
different next time in order to attain a better
result in the future. It is important to note
that trust is required in order to have an open
and honest discussion about the good, the
bad, and the ugly of the project. If you have
not built trust with your team, you will
likely get false information from them. You
need the truth, even if it is ugly!

The idea of being fully responsible for yourself and
your future can be a scary one. It is much easier to
place blame on others and avoid accountability. It's
just that doing those things will mean that you are
letting yourself stand in your own way!!! Don't do
that. Don't allow the temptation of resistance stand
in your way. Don't let other people tell you that
you aren't good enough, or smart enough, or
tenacious enough. Only you can control you, unless
you decide to give control to someone else. The
following are what I recommend that you keep at
the forefront of your mind to stay in control of your
destiny.

1. You are not your brother's keeper and he is
not yours either. You are responsible for
yourself and your brother, sister, grown
child, or whatever is responsible for
themselves. Other people will not take care
of themselves until they feel that they have
to. Take a stand right now and decide that
you are going to focus on being in charge of

you. Work as hard as you need to in order to not be a burden on others!

2. The fair comes to town once a year. Other than that, there is not fair. Life has never been fair. To be honest, that is probably a good thing. I have deserved to be in trouble a number of times that I wasn't "caught." When people say that life is not fair, they are saying that they want life to be unfair in their favor. I don't want to get what I deserve. I want to get so much more than I deserve. Those who work their tails off are the ones that have the "unfair advantage" over others. Make life unfair in your favor by doing more than others and doing it smarter than they do.

3. Chance favors the prepared. I love the Boy Scout Motto: Be Prepared. The original motto was "Always Prepared." When I was young, I did my homework and studied throughout the six weeks. When it was test time, I didn't have to study because I had already studied. In college, starting my Sophomore year, I started my papers the day that they were assigned to me. I was done early. I didn't have the stress that many of my friends did because I had plenty of time to redo or revise or just go for coffee. When we start early and plan our success, we find that life is not actually that tough. Be prepared by starting now and working as if your deadline is just around the corner. Don't wait until the 11th hour and hope for

the miracle. Work hard now so that you don't need a miracle to save you!

4. You are not your khaki's! Too many people identify themselves as their company or their stuff. The quote, "You are not your khaki's" comes from *Fight Club*, the movie. When you can keep a healthy dose of separation, you realize that an event that does not go right is not the definition of your life. Instead, it is just an event. Treat it as such and move forward! Live your life in a growth mindset, realizing that every challenge is simply an opportunity to learn something new and become something more. You are not set as who you are today. You are the sum total of your choices and what you learn from your challenges.

5. Switch pathways as often as you need, but don't take your eyes off the end goal. If you know what you intend to accomplish for you life, don't give up on it. Stay focused on the freedom or the growth or the revolution that is your life's drive. Everyone hits obstacles in their path. When you keep you eyes on the end goal, the obstacles seem like slight detours or even speed bumps. When you keep your eyes on the obstacles, however, they are giant walls that are impossible to scale. When I learned to break a board with my hand in martial arts, at 9 years old, I learned to see the other side. I was taught to NOT focus on the board, but rather to focus on what lay beyond the board. That lesson

is critical to any person's success. Know what is on the other side and realize that the pain of the challenge is worth the victory that is ahead of you!

I wish you all of the best in your journey to success! I look back at the struggles that I have had over the last 16+ years of being in business for myself and I realize that each challenge held the seed of an equivalent or greater opportunity inside of it. I have learned to be thankful for the growth opportunities that I have been given. I have learned that I am who I define myself as. James Allen said, "As a man thinketh, so he is. As a man continues to think, so he remains." If you want to be more than you are right now, simply begin to think like the people who are already there. When your mind is right, right action can't help but follow. Right belief leads to right thoughts. Right thoughts lead to right attitudes. Right attitudes lead to right behaviors. Right behaviors lead to right results. Believe that you are destined for greatness. Believe it with all of your heart and reinforce it with the way that you talk to yourself. Do this every day, at least three times per day for the next 22 days. I would encourage you to read these 12 steps every month for the next year. Internalize them and make them a part of who you are. This will position you for achieving the greatness that you were made to achieve. You are great! You are a success! Never forget that!

"Every failure, every adversity, every heartache, brings with it the seeds of an equivalent benefit!"
-- Napoleon Hill

Never back down because things are tough. Always remember that it is the tough times that prepare you for the great times!

To Your Success!

Jody N Holland – Fellow Journeyer

ABOUT THE AUTHOR

Jody Holland is an author, trainer, entrepreneur, and keynote speaker. He has written more than half a dozen books and has developed dozens of training programs. Jody has made it his obsession to learn more so that he has more to offer his clients. His books are available on Amazon.com and many are available on Audible.com as well.

If you are interested in booking Jody as a speaker for your conference, you can find him on his blog at www.jodyholland.com.

Made in the USA
Columbia, SC
04 July 2023